Trump's Prophetic Destiny

A book by John Whitman
and Smith Wigglesworth

Chapters from Smith Wigglesworth's *Ever Increasing Faith* reprinted from public domain

Scripture quotations are from *The Holy Bible*, King James Version (KJV) and Scripture marked New International Version (NIV) is from

Holy Bible, New International Version®, NIV® Copyright ©1973, 1978, 1984, 2011 by Biblica, Inc.® Used by permission. All rights reserved worldwide.

First Printing, 2019
Printed in the United States of America

Contents

And the LORD answered me, and said, Write the vision, and make it plain upon tables, that he may run that readeth it. For the vision is yet for an appointed time, but at the end it shall speak, and not lie: though it tarry, wait for it; because it will surely come, it will not tarry.

-   Habakkuk 2:2-3

Author's Note

I didn't want to write this book.

I'm thrilled, humbled, and honored to write it, but see, I'm not the perfect guy for the job.

God called me to complete the book some time ago. He said "sit down and write what I am revealing to you; it is urgent."

For a good long while, I ignored His command. Then I learned the hard way that the Lord will not be avoided, controlled, or silenced. Not ever and certainly not in such a season as now. The more I ran from the idea, the more it forced its way into my head until it began to dominate my mind.

Like Jonah, I continued to run. I begged the Lord for some other calling, a different task.

I woke up one morning feeling like I was in the deep end of the pool with concrete blocks strapped to my feet. I was flailing, helpless, and finally beaten by my anxious mind, by the Lord's calling on my life. Broken. Sitting on my couch where I had passed out the night before, feeling rough from the evening's bad choices, I waited in silence for Him to speak. Nothing. Finally, I cried out to God.

"Lord, c'mon, I'm just a writer! I'm not a political pundit, journalist, preacher or prophet. I'm nobody."

"I didn't ask you what you were or were not. I'm telling you to write this book," He responded, "keep it simple, straightforward, and above all **be clear and tell the truth**. That is all."

"But what about the prophets, God?" I continued, "there are so many people better suited to this task, people who have walked in your calling as seers and prophets for years, Lord, why not have them carry out this word?"

"My prophets and seers have their own calling. This is yours. This revelation is not about them and it's not about you, it is about Donald Trump, America, and bringing my people together again to pray, to call out on her behalf, to support and uplift the nation to her rightful place of greatness."

Have I not used fishermen, tax collectors, prostitutes, and convicts to spread my word? Have I not shown you throughout history that I can and will use ANYONE to carry out the work of the Father, Son, and Holy Spirit? Be of strong courage, my son. Take faith in the stories of the apostles, disciples, the common men and women all throughout the Bible who have stepped out in belief to do my work. The rewards are plentiful, but the laborers are few."

Then it was quiet. The kind of silence where you could hear anything…and nothing. I continued to wait on the Lord and eventually He spoke again—this time in an audible voice.

"John, will you heed my call? Will you write my words and make them known?"

"Speak Lord, for your servant hears." (I Samuel 3:10)

There was work to be done and the writing was on the wall; it was time to share it with you and with anyone who would take the time to read it. God's words for America and Donald Trump's prophetic destiny as her leader.

I'm not a prophet, but I was given a prophecy.

- John Whitman, April 14, 2019.

Preface

In the pages ahead, you will learn not only about Trump's destiny as president of the United States of America, but also God's vision for the destiny of America herself. As our leader goes, so goes our country in many ways. The other side of that coin is often forgotten: as a nation's people go, so her leader goes, and so the nation goes.

It's easy to blame leadership for the problems we see. We want to point the finger at the president, but if we take a step back and look at the evidence in God's Word, we will find that it is the individuals that make up a nation and the leadership of that nation reflects the cultural and spiritual attitudes of her people.

Along with many fellow Christians, I am looking for God's affirmation on the upcoming presidential election and insight on the direction America is heading. I am maintaining faith and hope that Donald Trump will continue to make policy decisions that come closer to aligning with God's laws and the foundational truths of our country. For this hope to be fulfilled, I believe more than anything that followers of Jesus must begin to testify, prophesy, heal, and witness. The Holy Spirit is ready to awaken a revival in America to a scale that has never been seen before, but it doesn't necessarily start with Donald Trump, it starts with believers. Revival starts with you and I.

For too long, Christians in recent years have been ruled by a spirit of fear. God is calling us to rebuke fear in Jesus' name and instead to live in the spirit of freedom which is born of the Lord. He is calling us to let go of our insecurities and ego and all the ideas we have about self and instead to believe, pray and live without worry while winning the lost in His name.

We will look at why prophecy is so important to America's future and present.

I'm not a preacher, a theologian, or a seer. I'm simply a believer who was given prophetic visions from God. Through sharing my experience with you on these pages, I hope to show how we as Christians have a part in fulfilling the destiny of our country and her president in the upcoming days. If I'm successful, you will have renewed hope and courage and also insight on what you can do in your daily life to positively impact the destiny of Donald Trump and your own walk with the Lord.

The atmosphere surrounding America is slowly shifting and it's changing for the good. Evil spirits are being dealt with, the battlegrounds are being prepared and it will be a long and trying fight between the righteous and the demonic. On an individual citizen's level, a duel between fear and courage.

God is revealing his plans for Donald Trump and I will reveal what I have learned from the Holy Spirit's anointed visions and words given to me. God has made it plain as to why Trump is His choice for president now and in the upcoming years. We will examine the specific evidence of why Trump is God's president before looking at ways we can prepare to combat the enemy's tactics as Satan will be fighting us like never before in the days ahead.

Beyond the battlegrounds is the sweet and refreshing presence of the Holy Spirit that offers constant renewal, peace and wisdom to those who abide in it. I will offer 3 keys to accessing this presence on an intimate level, keys that help me every day and contribute to my receiving revelatory visions and words from the Lord. This will be exceptionally important as we pray for President Trump in the months to come. We want our prayers to be as powerful and effective as possible.

My dear reader, even if you are not a believer, hear the words of God: this is a wakeup call to America and indirectly, the world. The end of time is near and God is calling us to awaken, to spread what is truth with courage and without apology.

Remember, the Lord has given us a spirit of sound mind and of courage, not fear.

Introduction

"... for they received the word with great eagerness, examining the Scriptures daily to see whether these things were so. (Acts 17:11**)**

It's important to test the words you are about to read against Scripture especially when hearing prophecies and considering their validity and anointing. Test them against the Divine Prophecy, God's Word. To this end, I've included a piece from a man who was a prophet of Godly discernment and impeccable word, the late evangelist and faith healer, Smith Wigglesworth. Smith Wigglesworth was a prophet's prophet while remaining a prophet among the people, and his wisdom from God is still highly regarded and sought-out over seventy years after his departure into glory.

Coming from the background of a plumber by trade, Wigglesworth followed God's call and stayed living in His presence and grace throughout the rest of his life as a preacher and evangelist. God gifted Smith with a fulfilled calling that included healing and prophecy and an eventual reputation for wisdom and power based on his accumulated experience and intimate relationship with the Lord.

Please read Wigglesworth's words as both a guide and a warning in this introductory piece as you prayerfully and carefully consider the revelations and insight on the following pages of *Trump's Prophetic Destiny*.

The Gift of Prophecy
Smith Wigglesworth, from *Ever Increasing Faith*

Utterance in prophecy has a real lifting power and gives real light on the truth to those who hear. **Prophecy is never a mind reflection, it is something far deeper than this. By means of prophecy we receive that which is the mind of the Lord;** and as we receive these blessed, fresh utterances through the Spirit of the Lord, the whole assembly is lifted into the realm of the spiritual. Our hearts and minds and whole bodies receive a quickening through the Spirit-given word. As the Spirit brings forth prophecy, we find there is healing and salvation and power in every line. For this reason it is one of the gifts that we ought to covet.

While we appreciate true prophecy, we must not forget that the Scriptures warn us in no uncertain manner concerning that which is false. In 1 John 4:1

we are told, *"Beloved, believe not every spirit, but try the spirits whether they are of God : because many false prophets are gone out into the world."*

And John tells us how we can tell the difference between the true and the false, *"Hereby know ye the Spirit of God : every spirit that confesseth that Jesus Christ is come in the flesh is of God : and every spirit that confesseth not that Jesus Christ is come in the flesh is not of God; but this is that spirit of antichrist, whereof ye have heard that it should come."*

There are voices which seem like prophecy and some have got into terrible darkness and bondage through listening to these counterfeits of the true gift of prophecy. True prophecy is always Christ-exalting, magnifying the Son of God, exalting the blood of Jesus Christ, encouraging the saints to praise and worship the true God. False prophecy deals with things that do not edify and is designed to puff up its hearers and to lead them into error.

Many picture Satan as a great, ugly monster with great ears, eyes and a tail; but the Scriptures give us no such picture of him. He was a being of great beauty whose heart became lifted up. He is manifesting himself everywhere today as an angel of light. He is full of pride, and if you don't watch, he will try to make you think you are somebody. This is the weakness of most preachers and most men and women—the idea of being somebody!

There are none of us who are anything, and *the more we know we are nothing, the more God can make us a channel of His power.* May the dear Lord save us from all these pride side-lines—they are the devil's traps. True prophecy will show you that Christ is all in all, and that you are in yourself less than nothing and vanity. False prophecy will not magnify Christ but will make you think that after all you are going to be some great one. You may be sure that such is inspired by "the chief of the sons of pride."

I want to warn you against the foolishness of continually seeking to hear voices. Look in the Bible. Here we have the voice of God, who at sundry times and in divers manners, spake in time past unto the fathers by the prophets, and hath in these last days spoken unto us by His Son.

Don't run away with anything else. If you hear the voice of God, it will be on the line of the Scriptures of truth given in the inspired Word. In Revelation 22:18, 19, we see the danger of attempting to add to or take from the prophecy of this Book. True prophecy, as it comes forth in the power of the Spirit of God, will neither take from nor add to the Scriptures, but will intensify and quicken that which already has been given to us of God. The Holy Ghost will bring to our remembrance all the things that Jesus said and did. True prophecy will bring forth things new and old out of the Scriptures of truth and will make them living and powerful to us.

Some may ask, *"If we have the Scriptures, why do we need prophecy?"* The Scriptures themselves answer this question. God has said that in the last days He will pour out His Spirit upon all flesh, "***and your sons and your daughters shall prophesy***." The Lord knew that in these last days prophecy would be a real means of blessing to us, and that is why we can count on Him giving us, by means of the Spirit, through His servants and His handmaids, true prophetic messages.

Paul wrote at the commandment of the Lord, "Let the prophets speak two or three, and let the others judge. If anything be revealed to another that sitteth by, let the first hold his peace. For ye may all prophesy one by one, that all may learn, and all may be comforted." If you are not humble enough to allow your prophecy to be judged, it is as surely wrong as you are wrong. **Prophecy has to be judged.** A meeting such as this one that Paul suggests would certainly be the greatest meeting you ever had. Praise God, the tide will rise to this. It will all come into perfect order when the church is bathed and lost in the great ideal of only glorifying Jesus. **Then things will come to pass that will be worthwhile.**

We read in the Revelation that the testimony of Jesus is the spirit of prophecy. You will find that true prophetic utterance always exalts the Lamb of God.

No prophetic touch is of any good unless there is fire in it. I never expect to be used of God till the fire burns. I feel that if I ever speak, it must be by the Spirit. At the same time, remember that the prophet must prophesy according to the measure of faith. If you rise up in your weakness, but rise up in love because you want to honor God, and just begin, you will find the presence of the Lord upon you. Act in faith and the Lord will meet you.

May God take us on and on into this glorious fact of faith, that we may be so in the Holy Ghost that God will work through us on the line of the miraculous and on the lines of prophecy, where we shall always know that it is no longer we, but He who is working through us, bringing forth that which is in His own divine good pleasure.

Chapter 1

God's President

Let every soul be subject unto the higher powers. For there is no power but of God: the powers that be are ordained of God.
Romans 13:1 (KJV)

Donald Trump as president scares us.

For some of us anyway, it's an idea that feels uneasy. God has positioned Trump in this way and during this hour because He wants to once again establish the fear of God in a nation that could be great again. Yes, it's true that Trump is unpredictable. He is volatile. But he came in and campaigned his way and won. He is symbolic of the future of politics which will be more open to God's will rather than the will of political parties and corporations' lobbyists and campaign donations.

We are entering a new generation of political positioning which is making available for the first time in many, many decades probably even over a century, the possibility of true and lasting positive change in our nation.

I prophesy that America is in the midst of birthing pains. It is the birth of a revival at the most unlikely of times and beginning through perhaps the most unlikely of persons.

Donald Trump is God's wake-up call to America.

God is activating prophetic words to our nation in order to birth a generational revival. When we believe, repent, pray, and act in faith, He is promising to meet us with revelation, healing, and a sweet presence of holiness that will spread across this country if we would but accept these four initiatives and believe in the power therein.

It all begins with a level of belief, a type of faith that manifests itself in action on a daily basis. It is not enough to be able to argue and debate and defend your beliefs, they must be seen in action for the fruit to truly ripen and bring forth beautiful change in the world.

What good is it, my brothers and sisters, if someone claims to have faith but has no deeds? Can such faith save them? Suppose a brother or a sister is without clothes and daily food. If one of you says to them, "Go in peace; keep warm and well fed," but does nothing about their physical needs, what good is it? (James 2:14-16) NIV

In order to show God's compassion to a hurting country, to a dying and lost world, we need to show compassion ourselves to everyone and anyone we encounter on a daily basis. *Our faith will be seen by our love for others.* This is a practical step. This is a wonderful expression of our strong belief in the Lord's promises.

Brothers and sisters, prophets and seers, evangelists and preachers, it is not enough to believe with the intellect in this current environment. A spiritual war is raging. The multitudes are relying on us. God is calling us to step out and feed the hungry, to heal the broken, to prophesy and to physically help people every opportunity we get. And if we start to pray in this way, if we start to say, "Lord, show me the broken, show me the people you want me to help TODAY."

If we cry out in His name and ask for His compassion to be manifested through our lives in our sometimes mundane, daily existence, we will begin to see the truth of this promise. We will begin to receive the blessings that accompany obedience to Christ's calling and commands. Then we will begin to experience believing from our heart, not just our head.

If any of you lacks wisdom, you should ask God, who gives generously to all without finding fault, and it

will be given to you. But when you ask, you must believe and not doubt, because the one who doubts is like a wave of the sea, blown and tossed by the wind. That person should not expect to receive anything from the Lord. Such a person is double-minded and unstable in all they do.
—James 1:5-7 NIV

Seek out the Lord's wisdom in FAITH. Don't go into prayer with the expectation that God is not going to hear you or is not going to answer your prayer for wisdom and guidance. Come to Christ in the full confidence that through HIM all things are possible!

He will provide you with the wisdom and guidance needed to act out your belief in His power. By praying with faith, you will be given the power of God to live and light the way for the lost.

This is the beginning of your own personal revival! Call on the Lord for wisdom daily!

New Wine

And he spake also a parable unto them; No man putteth a piece of a new garment upon an old; if otherwise, then both the new maketh a rent, and the piece that was taken out of the new agreeth not with the old. And no man putteth new wine into old bottles; else the new wine will burst the bottles, and be spilled, and the bottles shall perish. But new wine must be put into new bottles; and both are preserved. Luke 5:36-38

I saw the beginning of spring, grass sprouting bright green in patches, verdant buds on trees, and I heard the flurry of activity from the birds as the sweet smell of life blew in through my office window.

The Lord revealed to me that we are making way for a new beginning, a new generation of prophets and prophetesses proclaiming the truth of the promises they've been given. They will reclaim their God-given birthright to live in a country that seeks the higher level reality of Jesus Christ. A country that rests without fear in his promises, that truly desires to bring Heaven to earth.

The Lord is giving new words to new believers and they are as valuable as the words given to veterans and generals of the faith. It is not good for the Body of Christ to lean solely on the words and faith of the preachers and prophets, but also recognize and hear the voice of God through the babes in Christ.

The youth, the new believers are the flag bearers of Christianity in America for years to come. This is where we must place our new wine. This is where the buds of spring are beginning to burst forth and sing their song of praise.

Rejoice in the work of Christ! Rejoice and respect the words of the young prophets and prophetesses!

Change We Can Trust

The Kingdom of Heaven awaits and we can begin to show people what that means right now, right here on earth.

But it requires change.

It requires a deep trust in the Lord's plan and in his mysterious ways. The new beginning requires obedience and purification. Just as Jesus in telling the parable in Luke illustrates, if you put new wine into the old bottle, the bottle will break and both the bottle and wine will be wasted.

Renew

The Holy Spirit is urging us to be renewed in spirit, mind and body so that we can handle the new wine (change). America is not quite ready, and we must search inside ourselves as individuals and see where the Lord is convicting us to change and be better.

Where is God urging us to purify our lives or asking us to do more? Spend some time in devotions today, and see what the Holy Spirit points out to you.

You can't experience the new beginning in Christ while you are doing or living the same old way you have been. The same is true for America, God is using Donald Trump in a powerful way to prepare the new wineskins for the move of the Holy Spirit!

God's Wisdom during Election Season

It's easy to get anxiety during election season. You see the different candidates and read about what they stand for (or don't) and there is a tendency to think about what if this person were elected. What damage would it do to our country, etc.? This kind of thinking is natural, but unnecessary.

Remember that God holds the world in His hand, including America. He looks out for the sparrow and He will watch over you. There is a solution to worry and anxiety during this season. That solution is prayer. Turn off your TV, stop reading the political blogs for a while and spend some time with the Lord. He promises to remove your worries and He will come through on that promise if you would just take the time to ask. Take the time to pray about what worries you.

Visions of America's Spiritual Destiny

Several days ago, the Father touched me and I began to see more clearly what He has in store for America and Donald Trump. My illusions of self-importance fell away and I opened my eyes and arms toward the heavens in **humble repentance.** "Forgive me Lord, for the sin of pride, for the false belief that this is about me."

I felt a burden lifted from my mind but also my body. My mind was clear. It is amazing how getting right with God affects even our physical being. I began receiving visions.

I saw beautiful, ornate houses—not too fancy, but classy and brilliantly designed—on street after street and I was reminded that God was bringing America home again. He is making her great again for sure. He is preparing for us a wonderful home in Heaven, God's Kingdom.

Toxic Beliefs

For the rest of the day I fasted and my body began to get rid of toxins not only physical but spiritual. The negative attitudes and beliefs that prevented me from accessing the Holy Spirit's wonder-working power fell away. The lies from the enemy that poisoned my mind and kept me from experiencing the purity and goodness of the presence of God were revealed and left behind.

The evil spirit of disbelief was completely crushed by the understanding that even these visions were evidence of fulfilled prophecies from God. His divine word coming true in His time. The Holy Spirit had promised me just two days previous that he would begin to give me visions, that he would bless me with creativity I had not known before.

Divine Nature

How powerful is the miracle of God's promises coming to fruition! We shouldn't be surprised as the Bible spells it out for us in the following Scripture:

Whereby are given unto us exceeding great and precious promises: that by these ye might be partakers of the divine nature, having escaped the corruption that is in the world through lust.
2 Peter 1:4 (KJV)

Wow! We can be partakers of the divine nature and escape the corruption, the lust of the world. The lust of worldly desires, ambitions, and excess—we can be free of all of this by God's "exceeding great and precious promises."

That is powerful! And then in Corinthians:

For all the promises of God in him [are] yea, and in him Amen, unto the glory of God by us.
2 Corinthians 1:20 (KJV)

With the increase in creativity, the Lord gave me a mandate. He said, **"You must prophesy to bring forth obedience. You must prophesy to bring forth repentance and you must prophesy to bring forth prayer. Then shall your nation see revival. Now go and tell the others to prophesy in similar faith with humility and courage. This nation will once again find her true purpose through my blessing."**

After hearing this mandate, I was given a vision of a neon sign, like a billboard along the highway reading, *"And ye shall know the truth, and the truth shall make you free."* John 8:32 (KJV)

It dawned on me then that I would be free when I lived my truth, and my truth was the Lord's command to prophesy regarding Donald Trump and America in this current season and in the upcoming election season. When I obeyed and lived out the truth God had given me in this hour, I found myself experiencing a freedom that brought tears to my eyes and joy to my soul.

Friend, Christian, PLEASE live in the truth of God's word for your life. Right now, when you begin to let go of the ego and turn to your truth, you can experience the feeling of the burden falling off your back, the shackles dropping from your wrists and ankles and you will move with a light step and firm purpose unconcerned with the world's opinion.

God's Voice

The same day, I was walking back toward my office from the bathroom and the door was inexplicably closed and apparently locked from the inside. I tried the handle with no success. *Maybe something was stuck.* I turned the handle once more, not even stopping to wonder why it was shut. It was indeed locked.

I knocked on the door and the handle turned and the door swung open slowly. I walked inside expecting to see a family member, but these was not a soul to be seen. Nothing. No one.

Then I realized it was God. He was showing me once again that He is present in our daily (sometimes seemingly mundane or boring) existence.

*"Ask, and it shall be given you; seek, and ye shall find; **knock, and it shall be opened unto you**:For everyone that asketh receiveth; and he that seeketh findeth; and to him that knocketh it shall be opened."* Matthew 7:7-8 (KJV)

His promises are all around us.

Praying Past Politics

If My people who are called by My name will humble themselves, and pray and seek My face, and turn from their wicked ways, then I will hear from heaven, and will forgive their sin and heal their land. (2 Chronicles 7:14)

It all starts with prayer. The most powerful of actions a Christian can take when it comes to defending and hoping and worrying and wanting, prayer. It always comes back to calling upon the Lord and trusting with an unshakable hope in His Word that he will fulfill the promises and answer that prayer.

The Undefeatable Weapon

One day I found myself wondering "what if?" What if I were this or that, or had this or that, or could speak like so-and-so, how much more could I do? How much more effective could I be if only…

Immediately, the Lord told me, "Let it go. It is enough to believe." And I did and I felt my faith continue to grow. I fell on the floor in my office and began to pray in tongues. The Holy Spirit's presence filled the room and I found myself in tears through the intense feelings of gratitude toward God for His love and mercy.

Powerless, I continued to cry out for more of His presence, more of his divine destiny to be revealed, to be poured out upon Donald Trump and America.

Powerful Prayer

As I was able to stand and walk again, I sat down in my desk chair and began to write. Satan began to attack right away with thoughts about some offense I had felt earlier in the day at the words of a brother. The power of conviction hit me like a fist to the stomach and I returned my focus to God.

It was at that moment I realized that my belief in His promises, my faith in the power of God had changed me. It had provided me with an undefeatable weapon in the spiritual battle of my mind. Faith had changed everything for me. I'm talking about a faith that allows me to truly sense and be aware of the Lord's presence at every moment of the day. I'm talking about a faith that lets me submit in obedience to the Holy Spirit's promptings even when (to my simple mind) it was regarding the simplest of things. Like knocking on a door or picking up a paper clip or even sitting down in a certain chair.

What I realized when I started heeding these directions from the Holy Spirit was that He was truly everywhere! He is all around us, in us, and through us! Believe it or not, this was a revelation that shook me to the core.

Experience the Holy Ghost

I knew intellectually that the Holy Spirit was all around (omnipresent as I'd heard it described) and I even believed it. But it was all head knowledge, not heart experience. Until this evening, I had not known the extent of the Holy Spirit's presence experientially. At first I was taken aback, but I began to relax and understand the gargantuan possibilities that this level of faith presented.

For one thing, it meant that I would have far more intimate encounters with the Holy Spirit than I could've imagined. All around me each day are signs of this truth. God's only requirement of me is that I obey and follow this truth out in real life and prophesy and encourage others to fall before the Lord in prayer for America. This is what will bring real and lasting change to our country, God's country.

And it doesn't stop there.

When you begin to recognize God in every moment, He brings your attention to the hurting, the insecurities of ego, the constant pain and offense that those who are attached to their ego face on a daily basis as they struggle for significance in an insignificant world. We are just passing through but God shows us that it is our job to bring the realities of Heaven and His power to a broken earth and a broken people, people who can still be saved and turn from their wicked ways—people who could be healed if we would not let our own self-importance to get in the way.

We've become too comfortable, too complacent. We weary of our work too soon. Our efforts are not rewarded instantly and we quit. Friend, we must return to God's Word with prayer and fasting, with prayer and supplication.

Do you trust that Donald Trump has been appointed to lead? Do you carry anxiety about the upcoming election? Are you worried about what direction America could be headed with a liberal president?

The answers, the remedies are in God's Word! Praise God and Glory to Jesus!

Chapter 2

Why America Needs Prophecy

And it shall come to pass afterward, that I will pour out my spirit upon all flesh; and your sons and your daughters shall prophesy, your old men shall dream dreams, your young men shall see visions:

And also upon the servants and upon the handmaids in those days will I pour out my spirit.

And I will shew wonders in the heavens and in the earth, blood, and fire, and pillars of smoke.

The sun shall be turned into darkness, and the moon into blood, before the great and terrible day of the LORD come.

And it shall come to pass, that whosoever shall call on the name of the LORD shall be delivered: for in mount Zion and in Jerusalem shall be deliverance, as the LORD hath said, and in the remnant whom the LORD shall call. (Joel 2:28-32)

On the servants and handmaids, God promises to pour out His spirit! Friend, that's a promise and a command to share what the Holy Spirit is doing.

There are people making money selling tuition for schools for learning prophecy and some of that is well and good, but brother or sister in Christ, hear me now: you don't need to wait for some level of education or experience to prophesy. NOW is the appointed time!

No Better Time than Right Now

In fact, there is no time other than now, you must open your mouth, write it down, put it out there. A dying world waits for you! They aren't waiting for you to finish school or have so many years' experience under your belt, they need you right now!

The Lord is calling out to the body of Christ to prophesy in this season. He is calling us to stand up and be counted as those of the prophetic, those of the unshakable belief that Christ showed us how to live and die in this world through God's Son, Jesus. We are being called to stand as those who still believe that Jesus is alive in Heaven and freely gives of the power that He demonstrated in His short time on Earth.

Why is prophecy so important? Because it is the way that Christians can share with the world the voice of

God as He is speaking in this current hour. *Prophecy is now!* It is fluid and when used with discernment, it is accurate, uplifting and even healing. Especially for a nation that is struggling with division and political and social strife, prophecy can be extremely valuable. There's never been a more important time to focus on prophecy.

God Still Values Prophecy

God entrusted prophets to write much of the Bible. If that fact doesn't tell you how much importance He places on prophecy, I don't know what will. But experience will help. When you receive a word from God and you prophesy and you experience the accuracy and the potential help that it brings the receiver, you will understand that yes, this truly is of the Lord.

Many want to dismiss prophecy as a gift from the past, something that is no longer relevant or useful. This idea couldn't be further from the truth. Trust the Lord and step out and as Smith Wigglesworth wrote, "Act in faith and the Lord will meet you."

Believe!

One word was the beginning of a long conversation and revelation from the Lord regarding the upcoming season of change and increase. That word was:

believe. It blew my mind that this alone would be the word that I was given to prophesy. Once again, I started to doubt and seriously reconsider writing or speaking the words I was hearing.

But I took God at his word and I believed.

Christian, son or daughter of the Lord, please hear me! As we come into a new season of hope and revival, a new season of economic growth and culture battles, a new season of victorious spiritual warfare, we must believe! We must trust the Lord at His word and step out in Faith to do what He calls us to do.

It's easy to fall into the selfish state of introspection where we internally criticize and judge and note our every flaw. We make up a million excuses why we should not. And of course this line of thinking turns into a special opportunity to judge and analyze others' faults and it all leads us to a state of disbelief. We are nothing on our own, but with Christ Jesus, anything is possible! Can you believe that promise?

Please believe!

I can do all things through Christ who strengthens me. (Philippians 4:13)

What is it that you do not believe you can do? What is that you don't believe you are qualified for or worthy of? Because it's not God's voice putting this disbelief in your mind. Disbelief is Satan blabbing nonsense in your ears because someone else won't listen— someone else is stepping out and hearing God's voice and believing in His promises found in the Bible. So, the old devil is knocking on *your* door. Shut him out by your firm belief in truth.

God is calling us to believe as we come up on the election season. As we enter a year where more and more, politicians and reporters and writers, journalists, and bloggers will lie and twist the truth, God is calling out to His people to return to the promises of the Bible. Return to the belief and faith in what you know to be true. Overcome your doubt by prayer and turning from your inward (*false*) self and upward to God. Clear away the fog of self-doubt, fear, and the shadows of negative thinking.

God's Ways are Not Our Ways

As I waited on the Lord to unveil His next word, I drifted off into a perfectly beautiful and restful sleep. It was the kind of sleep you didn't want to wake up from even when you had exciting plans for the day.

During my sleep, I dreamed I saw an eagle, a young eagle. It was tenderly, carefully stepping over the edge of his nest, taking a step off, slowly beginning to flap his wings, then quickly retreating back to the safety of his nest.

I saw the eagle start out and return several times before the mother bird gently nudged it forward into the air and the young eaglet began to gain his confidence, pulling out of the midair tumble and into graceful flight. God's artistic grace is what this scene reminded me of.

The air began to get damp and the sky started to get dark, signaling the certain onset of a thunderstorm. There was a tumult among the people who were strangely gathered around the base of the tree that was home to the eagle's nest. Sounds of bickering and shouting echoed about. Election season. Voting. Politics of people. The politics of a nation struggling to find itself again.

It was symbolic of the tumult surrounding our current president.

President Donald Trump

I saw the Lord touch him and continue to change him from within, and I saw him empower the nation to bring great and lasting revival throughout the world. The truth is clear and Trump is the man God placed in charge at this appointed hour!

They said he could not change! They said he WOULD not change! They said he could not lead! They said he was a sexist, a racist, and a homophobe! They said he was not a friend of the melting pot ideal that is America!

Friend, it is not true. The Lord has spoken and will continue to speak. God is not finished with Donald Trump just like He is not finished with America, just like he is not finished with you and me! Amen? We must wait on the Lord, we will learn as Americans that we must wait for the Lord God's timing. His will is always right, it's always fair, it's always just and true and no matter if it makes sense to us at the time or not, we must TRUST the LORD.

"To everything there is a season,
A time for every purpose under heaven."
Ecclesiastes 3:1

I saw President Trump continue to be convicted by God's righteousness and begin to turn from his vitriolic language in tweets and social media communication. I saw him continue to be more sensitive to and stand up against the increasing persecution of Christian faith both internationally and in our own beloved country.

Youth of the Nation

As a result, there grew the seed of change in our popular culture, our music, our movies, and our youth of the nation. Our young people began to bow under the conviction of God. They began to turn from drugs and online addictions and began to cry out for something new. Something spiritual. Not the new-age mumbo jumbo, but something real! Something they could BELIEVE in and live out.

In large numbers, the youth of America began to turn to Christ. Revival would soon break out.

There was a rise to embrace the Christian heritage of our forefathers and founding mothers. Men and women of faith who had the courage to defend their right to worship the Almighty One. Men and women, Americans who were willing to give up their lives for their family's freedom to love God and country!

All of this starting the swell of the water before the flood, the gentle uprising of earth where roots were forming, strengthening, gaining in size and reach before a massive growth and harvest takes place.

Clear Away the Fog

Following these visions, a strange sensation came over me and I recognized the presence of the Lord.

Colors were brighter, my soul and my mind were at peace. Friend, reach out and touch Jesus through your own belief and rest in His promises. Experience the presence of God—there simply is no better feeling.

When I woke up, I could see the path before me more clearly than ever before. Jesus had indeed touched me and said, "Clear Away the Fog." It was the last thing I heard before regaining my senses and understanding that true revelation had just been given.

I rejoiced and continued to wait upon the Lord's voice.

He revealed something next that transformed the way I thought about America, about Donald Trump, and about my own complete lack of credibility in relaying this information.

The Spirit of the Lord is Freedom, Not Fear

And I saw in my vision three blackbirds flying in various patterns above a neighborhood in a small town in America. It could have been any town. The birds were flying uninhibited, unrestricted by the laws of gravity and they had no care or worry about the concerns of the many people living in the neighborhood below.

They were simply free. Unafraid. It dawned on me that the Lord was calling us to fly away from our self-consciousness. He is calling us to prophesy in freedom which is the spirit of our Father in Heaven. Through this vision, God was telling me to rise above my fear and speak His words over the neighborhood, the town, the state, and the country.

The Spirit of Fear is Satan

How much are we sacrificing on the altar of insignificance? How many blessings are we giving up due to our negative self-talk? I want to know how many times we have missed out on powerful encounters with the Holy Spirit due to our own human weakness and fear.

Friend, the spirit of fear is of the devil, it is not of God. We must resist this spirit at every turn and instead live in God's presence with reckless abandon giving ourselves over to the spirit of freedom, healing, and restoration.

Chapter 3

Three Keys to Accessing God's Presence Daily

And he said, My presence shall go with thee, and I will give thee rest.
Exodus 33:14

God promises us to go with us, to allow us access to His presence and find peace within. That's a powerful promise!

What are three concrete actions we can apply to our lives right now that will allow us to access God's presence and help fulfill America's prophetic destiny through God's leader, Donald Trump?

Prayer. Start your day with prayer. Continue to pray throughout the day for wisdom and guidance or whatever the situation, pray. End your day with prayer. If you aren't praying as frequently as you could, you will notice a significant boost in your awareness of God's Presence when you begin talking to Him as much as you can.

Repentance. Get right with God. This is critical to enjoying God's daily presence. God is a holy God and as such will not tolerate the double life of those who call themselves Christians but behind closed doors, act without character. Maybe, you don't see it that way. Maybe it feels like just a little sin, a little vice, something that God could overlook.

I'm telling you from experience, if you want to experience the Holy Spirit in a more consistent, fresh way, look within and repent. Find out what it is that is in your heart that needs to be released to renew your spirit.

Faith. This is a patient faith, a strong faith. I'm talking about faith like an anchor that tethers you to God and His holiness. It's the way you remain connected to His perfect peace each day among the hustle and bustle of life. Faith will give you the strength to get past all the daily hurdles, the obstacles big and small that Satan uses to block us from receiving God's presence.

Avoid Petty Politics

Being overly concerned with the affairs of this world can impact our access to God's presence in negative ways.

It's tempting to take part in the increasingly hostile political discussions both online and in person and really put people in their place when they are wrong, but this is a mistake. I'm not saying you shouldn't stand up for what you believe and defend the leader of the country (especially in this day and age when people are making up terrible lies about Trump).

I'm saying be careful of your witness. What do I mean by that? I mean your testimony. Watch and safeguard your reputation as a Christian regardless of whether you are talking to a fellow believer or a lost person, always be on guard for Satan's subtle attacks on your character. Politics is a perfect playground for the devil. He will take full advantage of the emotional interest that we have in different social issues, the elections and voting process, the media and our country's future.

There's nothing wrong with being emotionally and intellectually invested in these national ideas and issues, but just don't hold them so close that you begin to believe that you have to be right in every discussion at the expense of your identity as a believer in Christ.

Be the Example

Instead of engaging in petty arguments about the latest scandal surrounding our president, be an example of someone who is trusting God and living in that higher level of Jesus' love and the Holy Spirit's presence. It's so easy to give into the anger that can be incited with all the muckraking journalism and outright fabrication of stories that defame the leader God put in place in our country. It's a trap.

There is no benefit to being right when you are arguing with someone who doesn't want to know the truth. I've heard it said that there is no sense in being the smartest person in a room of fools. Your best move is probably to avoid the foolish talk surrounding all the crazy news stories that come out on a regular basis to sell fear and divide our nation further. Live out your beliefs rather than arguing them when possible.

People will always be more influenced by what you do and how you conduct yourself in different situations than by what you say.

Get Involved or Don't Complain

On the other hand, it's not fair to get into arguments or complain about the negative press given Donald Trump if you're not going to get involved, research, read up on the truth, pray, and vote. It's a privilege we have in America that many countries do not have to be able to act as a democracy and vote for our leaders.

If you are not voting, then there's no need to talk about politics with anyone. Get involved and exercise your civic duty and vote for our nation's leaders. There are too many people sitting around playing Monday morning quarterback, criticizing our leaders without offering up any solution or effort on their own part. Don't be one of them.

A Prayer for Americans

A prayer for our citizens to once again begin to value the awesome privilege it is to live in a free country with a democratic government:

Lord, we recognize and thank you for the blessing of being able to live in this land. It's a land overflowing with beauty and opportunity and may the Holy Spirit convict us when we take it for granted.

Dear Jesus, please continue to impact the your of our nation to understand that we can't sit idly by and expect the nation to remain a great place to live.

Edmund Burke wrote, "The only thing necessary for the triumph of evil is for good men to do nothing." The point is, we must vote, we must participate in local and national affairs.

Thank you, Lord for your guidance and wisdom in our involvement in the political issues of our lifetime that influence future generations. Amen.

Chapter 4

The End of Abortion

Thou shalt not kill. (Exodus 20:13)

But Jesus said, **Suffer little children***, and forbid them not, to come unto me: for of such is* **the** *kingdom of heaven.* (Matthew 19:14)

Defend the Defenseless

We will never see the true potential of our country's greatness if we do not begin to treat our most helpless citizens with greater love.

All throughout Scripture we find the Love of God for the nation's children. His love has not changed. I declare in the name of the Father that the murdering of unborn children must not continue to be condoned in this country.

If we would ever come back to the Lord and be a strong nation, I decree in the name of the Lord that we must begin to defend the most defenseless citizens among us, our unborn children. How far we have fallen! Friend, it is almost impossible to believe where we are in terms of abortion policy in this country. Donald Trump has been called of God to be a catalyst for the change that will lead to the court system overturning the Roe v. Wade decision. Amen?

God is just and will not let a nation's wickedness go unpunished. Let us repent and release ourselves as a country from the shame and shackles of our senseless abortion policies.

National Culture Wars

There is a culture war taking place in our country right now. There is a large, but not majority group of people who wish to undermine and reduce the influence of God and Christianity in our country. In most cases, I believe this to be a misguided, good-intentioned mistake by American citizenry, but it is really a testament to the subtle, evil nature of Satan.

He is out to eliminate Christianity in our homes, schools and most of all, our country. He will not be successful so long as the body of Christ continues to wage spiritual warfare against him. As long as believers will bow their head and pray and seek the Lord while He may be found, we have a chance to reverse this trend of making America atheist.

Donald Trump is helping to reverse this trend namely by his Supreme Court nominations. We will see in the upcoming years, more conservative judges and justices, and along these lines, the political, spiritual and moral atmosphere of the country will begin to shift. Finally!

But we must continue to pray, to vote, to speak up against wickedness in our entertainment, education, and in our politics.

Churches role in politics (stand up, be steadfast)

There are some who would say that the church has no place getting involved or speaking about politics. I denounce this as a lie from Satan. We as the body of Christ must still fight evil where we see it, we must still stand up for the biblical commands and laws of God Almighty. It might be easier to lie in the shadows and be quiet, but that is not what Christ taught.

Even to the extent that he was hung on the cross for his worldview. He didn't hide away and keep the truth from the people. We need people in political power who understand this and who will stand up and defend Christianity when it is coming under more and more persecution by other religious groups and by an increasingly atheistic and materialistic society.

On the one hand this illustrates many of the signs that the end is near and that is exciting, but it is not time to throw in the towel and die. It is a season of revival in which we are going to take as many people to Heaven with us as possible. It is time for one last cry to God, one last trumpet blast to the people to wake up and see the truth.

Believe and lay up treasures in Heaven before it is too late! This world will not last forever but God's promises will. Sometimes this call to the people to repent and be saved necessarily involves speaking out and influencing the political stage and who is running the country in what direction.

Be Sober, Be Vigilant

Be sober, be vigilant; because your adversary the devil, as a roaring lion, walketh about, seeking whom he may devour: (I Peter 5:8)

Throughout the election season and the seasons beyond, it is of utmost importance to be sober and vigilant. Now when the Bible says sober, it's not only talking about sober from the influence of drugs or alcohol but also from the influence of popular entertainment in excess, internet usage in excess, anything that takes you away from experiencing God's presence. Because in the presence of the Holy

Spirit lies the superior reality that we can live in and teach others to live in and from which place we can bring others to a saving knowledge of Christ.

Clean Conscience

That ye put off concerning the former conversation the old man, which is corrupt according to the deceitful lusts;
And be renewed in the spirit of your mind; And that ye put on the new man, which after God is created in righteousness and true holiness. (Ephesians 4:22-24)

Renewing your mind and keeping it holy, clean and in righteousness is the way to perfect peace. And for the purpose of Donald Trump and the country's future, it is the most imperative directive from God to turn this nation around.

For coming to a renewal of mind means, cleaning your conscience and living in a way in which you need not have any secrets or worry about some scandalous report or commission being revealed. There is only one commission that matters and that is the great commission. To complete our mandate from God, we must turn from the old woman or man, the corruption, and the deceitful lusts to become a different man or woman all together.

It all starts with renewing the mind, and you can't do that if you are abusing drugs and alcohol. We need to be present with the Holy Spirit.

If our mind is clouded by substances, it will be hard to hear the Lord's calling, the gentle nudges that happen all throughout the day when one is living in accordance with God and abiding in the anointing power of the Holy Spirit. Not only does this hurt your walk with Christ, it indirectly hurts all the lost souls who would have come to know Jesus if you would have been alert enough to respond to the Holy Spirit's prompting which may have included talking to some poor sinner in the mall, the gas station, or just walking down the street.

I'd like to close this chapter with a prayer for Donald Trump, America, and all of us.

A Prayer for Donald Trump

Lord, please, hear us now. We desire to be renewed and start over with a clean and clear conscience. We decree in your name the binds of any evil spirits that plague and harass us be broken. We declare your victory over Satan and all of his demons, devils and evil spirits.

Lord, we pray for Donald Trump in this hour of pressure, this hour of heavy responsibility that the leader of the free world must carry. We thank you for your infinite wisdom and we trust that we are in your hands forever.

Dear God, thank you for all your love, all your blessings, and all your kindness to us as sinners and we pray for Donald Trump and our nation to turn toward you like never before. We pray that our country will once again claim her Christian heritage and her privilege as your blessed land. Amen.

Chapter 5

Emerging Prophets

But the anointing which ye have received of him abideth in you, and ye need not that any man teach you: but as the same anointing teacheth you of all things, and is truth, and is no lie, and even as it hath taught you, ye shall abide in him. (1 John 2:27)

You don't need teachers, you need the anointing. This is already been given to you and Christ teaches you through this anointing and prophecy to continue to abide in Him and He shall abide in you. Learn this with your heart and you will understand that you already possess the anointing.

Emerson wrote, "Do the thing and you shall have the power."

This same truth was promised by Christ long before Emerson was born, and His promises stand forever. You can access this power today, Christians!

We must come out of our shells and do the things that Christ promised we could and would do through the Holy Spirit's power. We must begin today, right now, and we will surely be amazed by the blessings and miracles that follow our obedience and courage to act on the anointing we've been given.

Crunch Time!

My friend, we have to be aware that the hour in which we are living is absolutely critical. It is crunch time on earth! It is time to demonstrate the Kingdom power and truth on a daily basis—a moment-by-moment basis! And the only way to do this is to be in a state of hyper awareness of God's voice. When you live in God's presence, you are under His voice throughout the day. Let me give you an example.

She is Hungry

The other day, I left the office at lunch time to go grab a salad from a fast food joint in town. As I got my salad, I felt God lead me to park and eat in the car instead of going back to the office to eat while I worked. This was interesting as I typically don't eat in my car nor do I like being away from the office for more than a couple minutes during busy times of the year which this was.

Anyway, I went ahead and drove to the Walmart right next to the fast food place and proceeded to prepare my salad with dressing and get ready to eat. Lo and behold, an apparently homeless woman wandered over toward my truck. Inside, I was actually a little nervous. She was staggering around somewhat clearly high on some kind of drugs. My window was down and my first response was to roll the window up as soon as I realized that , yes, she was indeed coming over to me.

God's Voice

But I heard God's voice audibly this time, *"Leave the window down. She is just hungry."* That was all He said, and it was all that was needed. I felt the conviction of the Holy Spirit and I simply put the lid back on my grilled chicken salad and I handed it out the window to the lady.

"Here," I said, "I just got this for you."

"Thank you mister. I am so hungry. God bless you."

I gave her a gospel tract and I drove back to the office. Why didn't I go back and get another salad you might ask? Well, again, God touched me in a subtle way and said, *"Go back to work. It's not time to eat. Take a small fast and be present with Me for the rest of your day."*

Praying and Fasting

Friend, I can't tell you how wonderful I felt that afternoon. I was so productive and in tune with the

Father. Words can't describe. Of course, it was uncomfortable at first when my stomach kept growling and I felt the pangs of hunger, but it did not take long before those feelings went away. In between office tasks, I was able to communicate so intimately with the Holy Spirit, it was as though He was right beside me, all around me. He was.

Two months later, I was in church worshipping with my family and the congregation. The pastor preached an amazing sermon about loving God and loving people and how our faith is known by our deeds. I was encouraged, uplifted, and inspired to go out into the world that week and testify and heal people and love them.

As my family and I were walking out of the auditorium, a lady grabbed my arm. She said, "Excuse me, Mister. You probably don't remember me but I met you in the parking lot of Walmart a few months ago. You brought me lunch."

"Of course I remember you!" I said.

She continued, "Well, at some point after eating that salad, I fell asleep on the park bench on Main Street and had a dream that I was going to hell and the only thing that could save me was in my pocket. I knew I didn't have any more drugs left so it wasn't that. But the reality of the dream was so scary and intense that

I searched the pockets of my jeans anyway and found this."

She held up the gospel tract I had given her which had the church's address on the back and was the reason she was there. She had been redeemed, healed of her drug addiction and now had a home in Heaven.

Immersed in the Miraculous

You never know what might happen when you walk in the presence of the Lord on a daily basis even in the most mundane of circumstances like the details of your typical nine-to-five day. It is always possible to go deeper in your faith in Christ and become truly immersed in the glory of the Holy Spirit.

When you become immersed and you are able to walk in it every day, you will see the miraculous become real in your life. You'll be watching for the opportunities to demonstrate the Kingdom of God and they will come to you without inhibition and in great abundance as promised by our Father in Heaven.

Go deeper with Christ from the starting point of being sober and vigilant.

The Importance of Faith in 2020

The Lord is rebuking the negative spirit of the pessimistic worldview that is invading our churches and our fellow believers. Yes, things have changed. Yes, there is a spiritual battle going on in high places and it is intense beyond measure. But it is not too big for God. We must be on the watch to maintain our faith in God's promises and not give into the cynicism of the end times.

There is simply too much to be done. Not only that, there are too many opportunities to see God at work and the Holy Spirit's influence even in the most dire of situations. Whether in national politics or in international affairs, rejoice to know and see that God is still in control. He is still God and He will always protect and help His children.

While the moral compass of our culture may seem to be broken, God's Word never is. He is steadfast, unmovable, a rock in times of trouble. Turn to him in faith when you are feeling depressed about the current state of affairs. In dark times, He will not leave.

Faith is the necessary ingredient to uplift and bring joy to a world that still has hope.

Chapter 6

A Good Old-fashioned American Revival

Wilt thou not revive us again: that thy people may rejoice in thee? (Psalm 85:6)

The hand of the Lord was upon me, and carried me out in the spirit of the Lord, and set me down in the midst of the valley which was full of bones, And caused me to pass by them round about: and, behold, there were very many in the open valley; and, lo, they were very dry.
And he said unto me, Son of man, can these bones live? And I answered, O Lord God, thou knowest. Again he said unto me, Prophesy upon these bones, and say unto them, O ye dry bones, hear the word of the Lord. Thus saith the Lord God unto these bones; Behold, I will cause breath to enter into you, and ye shall live: (Ezekiel 37:1-4)

Dry bones. This describes America's current spiritual state, unfortunately. It is high time to prophesy life and love into our leader, into our country! Lord, revive us again!

In the name of God, I declare and decree the onset of a revival such as we have not seen in this country. The Lord is ready to pour out his blessing upon us; rains of revival are set to flood America. Miraculous conversions will happen among the celebrities: movie stars, athletes, and politicians will turn from greed and other evils and claim the one true God.

The shift in our country will be traumatic for many, glorious for others. But one thing will be for certain and that is that all shall know Christ is the King and there never was another one more powerful or loving. Men and women will forsake the god of status and money and will instead begin to seek out what they can do to make the world a better place.

Wherefore he saith, Awake thou that sleepest, and arise from the dead, and Christ shall give thee light. See then that ye walk circumspectly, not as fools, but as wise, Redeeming the time, because the days are evil. (Ephesians 5:14-17)

People will turn in large numbers from addiction, pornography, and alcohol. The world shall begin to look to America as the rock of strength and the ideal place of faith and freedom that it once was.

To Think it Happened on Azusa Street

And it all started way, way back in 1906 (well, before then really) with William Seymour following the calling of the Lord and hosting meetings where the Holy Spirit's presence hovered and was felt for service after service for many years to follow.

The public criticized the minister and the parishioners. The crowds that gathered and witnessed healings, speaking in tongues, and all manner of miracles were ridiculed by the outsiders, but that didn't stop them from gathering. For nine years consecutively, the Azusa Street revival continued by the grace of God and the presence of the Holy Spirit.

People often condemn what they don't understand and few are those who would be willing to participate and join before criticizing, but plenty of people found Jesus in those meetings. Lives were changed. Generations were influenced by Seymour's willingness to heed the call of Christ and prophesy regardless of the reactions of the unsaved.

How many lives were touched, how many future criminals were redeemed, saved from a life of heartache and pain when they found Christ during those meetings?

Christians, 2020 is the year that could be your own version of the Azusa street miracles. You must believe. Love your neighbor as Jesus loves you, let your light so shine and see the work of Heaven on earth.

A Prayer for Revival

Let's close this chapter with a prayer for revival:

Holy Spirit, please fall upon me as I pray these words over the reader of this book, over the nation we call America, over our country's president, Donald Trump. Dear Jesus, please hear our cries for American revival! Please let us increase our faith and trust in you, in your love and holy power. Make us wholly devoted to spreading the news of Christ's finished work on the cross to all nations.

Lord, help us see the potential of living in a nation that is submitted and obedient to God's Word. Help us as individuals to repent, pray and exercise the faith needed to prophesy and cleanse our own lives, thus beginning the next great awakening here in America. Amen.

Chapter 7

Signs and Wonders

So Paul and Barnabas spent considerable time there, speaking boldly for the Lord, who confirmed the message of his grace by enabling them to perform signs and wonders.
Acts 14:3 (NIV)

Throughout our lives, if we choose to act on obedience to the Lord's calling, we will be resisted. Especially by the demons and the darkness on high. Satan's forces will conspire against us and try to bring us down by any means possible. It is essential to be prepared.

We won't always be ready. There are times when we get down or angry or frustrated and these are the moments when we are most susceptible to the devil's attacks. In those moments, you will find God if you but believe this and accept it as truth. Let me give you an example from my life just in writing this book.

Since I overcame my own insecurities at the outset of this project and I heeded the Lord's call for me to write these words, I have been attacked by all manner of temptations including procrastination and self-defeating thoughts of doubt. One such morning when I should have been writing, I was wandering around the house, picking up sundry items, doing dishes and generally feeling sad and depressed about my life and even this book. I thought, *no one cares, John, give it up and do something useful.*

As I was walking through the hallway back to my office debating whether to close up shop and leave or to try once more, I glanced down—it was almost invisible due to the color of the carpet—and I saw a paper clip. And I picked it up and looked at it and as I went to set it down on my desk, I heard these words almost as clear as an audible voice of God, "Hold it together, John."

If you are doing what you should be doing, God will help you with little reminders like this paper clip. He will offer encouragement and admonition from the strangest of sources and in the most unique of ways, but only if you are available and remain steady in the belief that He is there even in your darkest times.

It was just a short message, but so needed in that minute. Hold it together.

Signs

And Moses answered and said, But, behold, they will not believe me, nor hearken unto my voice: for they will say, The Lord hath not appeared unto thee.
And the Lord said unto him, What is that in thine hand? And he said, A rod.
And he said, Cast it on the ground. And he cast it on the ground, and it became a serpent; and Moses fled from before it.
(Exodus 4:1-3)

How's that for a sign? Moses, even in his moment of self-doubt trusted the voice of God, did what was commanded and was given a valuable sign. He was feeling down and rejected and was beginning to perhaps underestimate God when the Lord reminded him of the power of God's presence.

Call unto me, and I will answer thee, and show thee great and mighty things, which thou knowest not.
(Jeremiah 33:3)

Remember to be open to God even during these times of frustration.

Pay attention to the signs from God that tell you if you are on the right track or not. When you are living in His Presence, you will see them all around you.

Stop Looking for Shortcuts

Patience, waiting on the Lord for His timing can be difficult and trying especially when you want results right now. Maybe you feel like the nation is in crisis and you wonder what is taking God so long to make changes? What is to be gained from all the moral decay we are seeing around us and all the lost souls without hope?

But that is when we must dig down and be honest with ourselves about what we are doing to bring the Kingdom of Heaven to earth. What is it that we are doing with all our time to make this world better? What have we done this week to bring lost souls to Christ? Are we scared to prophesy, too timid to speak the words of the Holy Spirit?

The Devil is Busy, Why Aren't We?

Brothers and sisters, stop looking for the quick way out. Stop looking for things to all of sudden change. We must change. Learn to love the process.

We must act differently. We must exercise our faith in Christ Jesus our Savior and step out and reach people. The devil is busy, why aren't we?

There is no easy way to put it. We must be diligent, there is no shortcut. Work harder for Christ as only this work will last.

In closing this chapter, I ask you to prayerfully consider the following poem by missionary, C.T. Studd:

Two little lines I heard one day,
Traveling along life's busy way;
Bringing conviction to my heart,
And from my mind would not depart;
Only one life, twill soon be past,
Only what's done for Christ will last.
Only one life, yes only one,
Soon will its fleeting hours be done;
Then, in 'that day' my Lord to meet,
And stand before His Judgement seat;
Only one life, 'twill soon be past,
Only what's done for Christ will last.
Only one life, the still small voice,
Gently pleads for a better choice
Bidding me selfish aims to leave,
And to God's holy will to cleave;
Only one life, 'twill soon be past,
Only what's done for Christ will last.
Only one life, a few brief years,
Each with its burdens, hopes, and fears;
Each with its clays I must fulfill,
living for self or in His will;

Only one life, 'twill soon be past,
Only what's done for Christ will last.
When this bright world would tempt me sore,
When Satan would a victory score;
When self would seek to have its way,
Then help me Lord with joy to say;
Only one life, 'twill soon be past,
Only what's done for Christ will last.
Give me Father, a purpose deep,
In joy or sorrow Thy word to keep;
Faithful and true what e'er the strife,
Pleasing Thee in my daily life;
Only one life, 'twill soon be past,
Only what's done for Christ will last.
Oh let my love with fervor burn,
And from the world now let me turn;
Living for Thee, and Thee alone,
Bringing Thee pleasure on Thy throne;
Only one life, "twill soon be past,
Only what's done for Christ will last.
Only one life, yes only one,
Now let me say,"Thy will be done";
And when at last I'll hear the call,
I know I'll say "twas worth it all";
Only one life, 'twill soon be past,
Only what's done for Christ will last. "

Only One Life, T'will Soon be Past
-C.T.Studd

The Nail clippers

What? know ye not that your body is the temple of the Holy Ghost which is in you, which ye have of God, and ye are not your own? I Corinthians 6:19 (KJV)

I looked down and saw a pair of fingernail clippers on the floor. The Lord spoke to me and helped me understand that the clippers symbolized taking care of myself and trimming the unnecessary from my life. Even when you are feeling low, it is important to maintain your body which is the temple of the Holy Spirit. Ask the Lord to guide you in learning what negatives you can cut from your life.

We've Become Too Comfortable in this Hour of Need

Reader, the good news is that Donald Trump will be reelected and this will represent the positive change of Christian values once more being reinstated. The bad news is, we've grown fat and lazy as the body of Christ. All around us, people are perishing. Doomed to Hell often by their own ignorance, but also from a lack of witnessing on the part of Christians.

There needs to be an increased sense of urgency among God's people. This is the hour He has pointed to as the season of change, redemption, and expediency. Our heart must begin to burn with a passion for winning the lost. A passion for seeing God's grace and mercy in action among our neighborhoods, our workplaces, towns, cities and America.

Consider this passage from God's Word:

I solemnly charge you in the presence of God and of Christ Jesus, who is to judge the living and the dead, and by His appearing and His kingdom: preach the word; be ready in season and out of season; reprove, rebuke, exhort, with great patience and instruction.
2 Timothy 4:1-2

Friend, please believe now is the time. Pray with me. Ask God to bless you and convict you with a sense of discomfort that makes you move from your status quo life and seek more of Him. To leave your nest of familiarity and cry out for that intimate encounter with Jesus. It comes through the Father, through following his mandate to seek out and save and heal those who are lost.

Say not ye, There are yet four months, and then cometh harvest? behold, I say unto you, Lift up your eyes, and look on the fields; for they are white already to harvest.

*And he that reapeth receiveth wages, and gathereth
fruit unto life eternal: that both he that soweth and he
that reapeth may rejoice together.*
*And herein is that saying true, One soweth, and
another reapeth.*
John 4:35-37

Notice what the Bible says in this passage. "Lift up
your eyes, and look on the fields; for they are white
already to harvest." The time is here and do not delay
in gathering the harvest for Christ because you are
building an eternal future, a life in which you will be
repaid for your efforts for all of eternity.

Remember this when you find yourself too wrapped
up in the decisions of President Trump and the
political machine.

Instead of being overly focused on the politics, let
yourself be aware. Look for the signs and wonders
from the Lord. They'll be there if you'll only wait on
Him and pay attention.

Prayer for Signs and Wonders

Dear Lord, make Yourself more and more real to us
through the presence and power of the Holy Spirit.
May we be aware of your signs at each moment so
that we can demonstrate the wonder of your power to
those that would believe, amen.

Chapter 8

Satan's Sabotage

When anyone hears the message about the kingdom and does not understand it, the evil one comes and snatches away what was sown in their heart. This is the seed sown along the path.

Matthew 13:19 (NIV)

Put on the full armor of God, so that you can take your stand against the devil's schemes.

Ephesians 6:11 (NIV)

There are a couple of ways in which the devil will aim to deceive us in the upcoming election season and also the days and years to follow. Of course, when you think about it, there are MANY ways in which Satan will try to deceive us, but for the sake of discussion regarding the destiny of Trump and America in the days we are in, we will stick with two exceptionally subtle and effective techniques.

One is to blind us from the truth or confuse us so we don't understand. This is a tactic he employs frequently on non-believers in an effort to prevent them from coming to know Christ.

He'll use stories of hypocritical Christians, evidence against the truth of the Scriptures, and just plain ignorance in order to keep the unbeliever in the dark. Because as long as they don't cry out to God and ask for knowledge, ask for the signs, ask for the revelation of His truth and presence, they remain ignorant of the benefits, and they remain ignorant of the evidence of Christ's love.

Deception of Self-importance

The next scheme that Satan uses is one we'll get into more detail about later on, but for now, let's call it self-importance. The devil wants us to be offended all of the time so we think that other people are wrong, and we are right.

Self-importance does two very negative things that influence our country and her future. When we begin to see ourselves as separate, better than or even a victim of the others, we lose sight of what is good for the whole group.

Secondly, when we are focused on ourselves, we are not focused on God and His power to save and heal a people and a nation. Through deception, Satan makes us think that we are at the center of the universe, and everything surrounds us and happens through our perspective of the world. It's an ego-centric ideal that makes us completely lose sight of the Lord and our fellow brothers and sisters.

Remember this at the end of the day:

Satan is very much against Donald Trump being reelected and for many of the reasons outlined in chapter one. We must be on guard and prepared more than ever before so that we can be proactive instead of reactive in the spiritual warfare ahead.

Consider the following Scripture:

But if our gospel be hid, it is hid to them that are lost: In whom the god of this world hath blinded the minds of them which believe not, lest the light of the glorious gospel of Christ, who is the image of God, should shine unto them.
For we preach not ourselves, but Christ Jesus the Lord; and ourselves your servants for Jesus' sake.
For God, who commanded the light to shine out of darkness, hath shined in our hearts, to give the light of the knowledge of the glory of God in the face of Jesus Christ.
But we have this treasure in earthen vessels, that the excellency of the power may be of God, and not of us.
(2 Corinthians 4:3-7)

We are COMMANDED to let our light of the knowledge of the glory of God shine! This isn't a request or a suggestion for improvement, friend! This is a mandate from the Lord! Is your self-consciousness worth disobeying the Lord?

Is your anxiety over what other minds think of you more important than glorifying God and leading others to Christ? Oh, I pray for Americans to continue to let go of their ego and let God take the reins, "that the excellency of the power may be of God, and not of us."

Experience this miraculous change in mindset and defeat Satan at every turn!

No Self (denial of self-importance)

Then he called the crowd to him along with his disciples and said: "Whoever wants to be my disciple must deny themselves and take up their cross and follow me. (Mark 8:34)NIV

With my senses sharp and clean as the edge of a chef's blade, I was given the following impartation: America, known for her rugged individualism, must release her sense of pride and become humble before the Lord. Her citizens must drop their facades and masks and their selfish desires to be more (or in some cases less) than what the Lord God Almighty has designed them to be. The Creator has spoken.

I said, "Lord, what do you mean by this? I receive this word, but what am I to put into practice and share with others?"

"Patience, my son."

I waited several minutes and He spoke again.

Our True Purpose

"Americans will lay down their careers, their goals for individual achievement, awards, accolades, and they will begin to follow the calling of God. They've known God's purpose for them since they were children, but through the years they have been indoctrinated with false information about the realities of life. Their true purpose has been buried, long forgotten. They were not taught that there is a superior reality to this one."

"Heaven, right?" I asked.

"Yes, Heaven, but something more, something now; there is a reality that can be and should be experienced here on Earth by more believers. By all believers! It requires the setting aside of your sense of self—your constructed identity as Donald Trump or

John Whitman or whatever your name and occupation and interests, you have to throw that away for this season of change!"

Dying to Self

The Lord was revealing to me the importance and crucial responsibility of Christians to live and walk in His presence. To soak in His spiritual being. To become more like our Savior. This revelation would be part of the catalyst for change, but it requires giving up our attachment to everything earthly we know.

I am crucified with Christ: nevertheless I live; yet not I, but Christ liveth in me: and the life which I now live in the flesh I live by the faith of the Son of God, who loved me, and gave himself for me. (Galatians 2:20)

Rest peacefully in this biblical promise that we are already dead! We were crucified with Christ, which means we give up our earthly loves and live by faith. We are alive because Christ is alive and lives through us!

Friend, we are ALIVE when we live through God's holy presence! When we allow the Holy Spirit to work through us and heal and help and present opportunities to perform and witness miracles! Why are we short-changing our experience of God for inferior goals of bigger houses, nicer cars, and stronger reputations and resumes?

Faithfulness before Happiness

There is nothing to fear, nothing to lose except that which will be lost some day anyway. Please, the Lord is calling us to a higher level of living. This great country of ours can again turn and chase after God instead of man, pursue faithfulness and holiness instead of only happiness.

God revealed to me that our country and our president must overcome one obstacle, one sinister trick of the devil in order to get this snowball of revival rolling across the land. One small deception that makes us vulnerable to our enemies in this upcoming season of vicious spiritual warfare:

Fear.

Christians, we are being too secretive. Pray for strength and courage. Please speak out about the wickedness in high places. We must become explosive as a people and as a nation, we must bring the firestorm of revival that God promises us if we will only follow his directions!

For God hath not given us the spirit of fear; but of power, and of love, and of a sound mind. (2 Timothy 1:7)

If God is not the one who gave us a spirit of fear, it can only be one other source, Satan. That's right, I am seeing an increase in the spirit of fear sweeping through our neighborhoods, our towns, cities, and our country. President Trump is the leader who will begin to release the spirit of fear from himself and make godly decisions. He will begin to turn this country away from the fear of political opinions and the fear of offending every little group of people the world over and begin to strengthen and emphasize the Christian ideals of our nation's birth.

More Faith, Less Fear

We are not called to be fearful, paranoid, or worried about every (often extreme) negative event that could come our way. Living a risk-averse life is unbelievably devastating to our faith. More faith, less fear. That is the mantra for 2020 and beyond. Today is the day for taking back our country's foundation.

God is calling us to trust in him, to have faith just as big (small) as a mustard seed and move mountains. What's interesting about the above verse from Timothy is the idea that a sound mind means a lack of fear. The Lord is promising us that we can and should have a sound mind free of fear and full of power and love.

Tap into the Power of Love

What if we started questioning our motives more often? I mean what if when we did something or didn't do something, we asked ourselves: was this decision made out of fear or love? Are we of sound mind and full of power or are we living out of a spirit of fear?

The spirit of fear that pervades our country in this season is too frequently IGNORED. It is our duty to prophesy and speak out against this spirit. As Scripture clearly points out, it is not a spirit from God. That means it is a spirit that is to be fought against. We must take down the notion that Christianity is a belief system for weak-hearted and weak-minded people. It is not so. And it is high time we begin to tap into the power that is freely available through God's promises and His presence through the Holy Spirit.

Sons and daughters, sisters and brothers in Christ, now is the season for immersing ourselves in the Lord's power and presence.

Chapter 9

The Spiritual Awakening

And that, knowing the time, that now it is high time to awake out of sleep: for now is our salvation nearer than when we believed.
Romans 13:11

I woke up and my heart was pounding through my chest.

It was a nightmarish sensation accompanied by the feeling that I was floating, maybe 10 feet from the ground, but still in a laying down position.

It was an unexpected vision and I wasn't quite awake so there was a dreamlike quality to it that burned itself into my mind. My heart still throbbing, I begin to slowly spin midair, ever so slowly turning 360 degrees and then stopping. When I stopped, I opened my eyes instinctively as if God was saying it was time to wake up, the vision is over.

Listen to My Words

But it was unpleasant when I opened my eyes, my heart was still beating too fast and I was sweating and felt somewhat nauseous, so I closed my eyes again and immediately the floating sensation and the slow rotation resumed.

"Lord, what are you trying to tell me? What are you showing me and what should I do with this vision?"

Then I was jolted awake again and this time I sat up straight in bed. I heard knocking. A loud knocking sound, but it wasn't coming from downstairs or outside, it was a knocking on my heart. It was Jesus saying, "Let me in and listen to my words."

"Awake, awake, put on strength, O arm of the Lord; awake, as in the ancient days, in the generations of old." (Isaiah 51:9)

So I relaxed and listened knowing now for sure that this vision was of God and not just a strange dream.

We are being summoned from on high, a voice from Heaven is declaring our responsibility and our duty to AWAKEN! It is time to begin to prophesy the words of our Father. We have slumbered too long and now it is the season of awakening to the glorious presence and revival of spiritual encounters. There has not been enough godly noise.

Bring the Kingdom to the Streets

Plenty of worldly fears and celebrity nonsense covers our news websites and magazines, but what demonstrations of the Kingdom on the streets? Where are the revivals starting in a church somewhere that spread throughout a town, throughout a city?

Where is the passionate crying out and yearning for the Lord's purposes? Oh, that we would awaken to what is possible! Let us fall down and pray for one another, pray for our leader at this hour, Donald Trump, pray for our country, America! It is time for another reformation in God's name. He is knocking. We are ordained for this mission.

The slow rotating sensation I was feeling, was symbolic of God's commandment to us to spread his word into all nations, all corners of the earth. Not just one specific area.

Go Forth Into Battle

Our obedience in this area will come to define America in the coming years and generations. Our commitment to spreading the truth, light, and healing power of God's word is the key to unlocking glorious revival for our children and their children to come. Will we heed the call in this season of hope and change? Will we awaken from our comfort zones and go forth in this battle of spiritual forces and take the side of Heaven's strategies? Will we abandon our sense of self for the superior reality of God's Kingdom on earth as it is in Heaven?

One issue that inhibits this march into righteous demonstrations of God's power is our own selfish actions.

Sin in the Church

"Awake to righteousness, and sin not; for some have not the knowledge of God: I speak this to your shame."
1 Corinthians 15:34

It's a tough word from the apostle Paul, but it is critical and urgent that we receive this word and act on it. In this day and age, we are seeing an increase in sin in the church and a decrease in moral standards from the Body of Christ. Friend, we must reverse this trend immediately! We must be above board in our behavior and our example as we represent Christ to the unsaved.

Restore Righteousness in the Church

We'll never experience the downpour of revival and a return to an intense focus of America on her divine purpose until we begin to restore the righteousness of the Church. It won't happen. America longs to flourish again; God is willing it! Will we cleanse our own hearts in this hour? Will we continue to bear the fruit of the spirit and the Holy Spirit in our daily walks of life? Will Christ be seen in our behavior, in our actions even when we don't know if someone is looking?

The answers to these questions of us as individuals help to determine America's prophetic destiny. Consider these prophetic words from the book of Daniel:

And such as do wickedly against the covenant shall he corrupt by flatteries: but the people that do know their God shall be strong, and do exploits.
Daniel 11:32

Take a minute and ask yourself, will you be corrupted by the flatteries and temptations of this world? Or will you remain righteous and choose to know God and perform wonders in His name?

Friend, the choice is clear. In the midst of our worldly travels, it may not always be an easy choice to make, but call on the Lord and He will give you the strength and resolve to know Him and follow Him. The rewards of knowing God far outweigh the temporary pleasures of the world's flattery.

Let's pray.

A Prayer for Personal Spiritual Awakening

Lord Jesus, touch each one of us today and remind of us of your power. Lord, we call out to you and ask for our own personal spiritual awakening in our daily life—starting today! Christ, please transform us through a fresh awareness of your presence.

Help us to overcome our failings. When we fall into sin or make a mistake, help us to remain awake enough to recognize our error and make it right and turn from any sinful way immediately!

For we know the rewards of knowing You and living righteous in Your sight include demonstrations of power and leading lost souls to Your Kingdom. We want this power and this lifestyle more than anything, Lord. Please awaken us and show us more!

Chapter 10

Unexpected Change

And suddenly there was a great earthquake, so that the foundations of the prison were shaken: and immediately all the doors were opened, and every one's bands were loosed.
Acts 16:26

God has revealed that Donald Trump will be elected for a second term.

This will cause half of Americans to be upset. Among Christians, some will lament his bad behavior and clearly un-Christlike behavior while others will recognize that God is in control and God is using Donald Trump to begin to roll a snowball of change. A slow-burning reckoning that will start the painful turn of our country toward God. The one True God.

Where are We Headed with Donald Trump at the Helm?

She is headed back to a more primitive time period in terms of culture. We are heading back to our roots, our Christian faith, our freedoms, and our nation's original goal: which was to remain free of government tyranny. Slowly, this progress has been eroded through numerous different causes, reasons, and excuses.

God is love, God is good and God is love. And that is the bottom line of all we need to remember. He will walk with you and hold your hand, he is everything you need and everything you will want in the coming days.

Make me whole again, Lord. Make me whole. Teach me to pray, Lord, teach me to pray in a way that is so powerful, so impacting, so effective in spreading your word, spreading your love to the nations and the country and the world and the universe, that one staggers under the might of it.
It's a power so true that it cannot be defeated.

Freedom of Religion

It is important because for once, change is not just a slogan. For once, change can be real and this is the time it begins and it is real and for the first time in a long time we are addressing sticky issues like abortion and immigration. Freedom of religion.

America is under strain—similar to the strain of a rope being pulled in separate directions. The left pulling with all their collective, angry strength in one direction, and the right pulling with their scared, deadly reactionism in another and so far both sides are pulling so hard that we are down to a couple of threads. Most of us live on those threads.

God, teach us to live with understanding and patience with those who hold opposing viewpoints. Teach us that fear motivates extreme behavior and polarizing rhetoric. Let us not be pulled into the useless arguing but instead, let us focus and proclaim your promises for our nation.

Many Will Turn From Their Sins

I proclaim the Lord's strength and supernatural power that we will see more and more people come to the Lord's saving grace, power and peace. That they will forsake their addictions, their violent video games, sexual fantasies and obsessions with all things unholy. They will come back to God and repent!

Trump will be among that number. He will change his ways and come to understand the division he is unnecessarily causing by his sharp, critical, caustic, and sometimes foolish words. He will understand for the first time in his presidency why so many hate him, and he will adjust his tactics and behavior accordingly. But this will not be enough for our God. This will not be the change in heart that Jesus came to bring. This will simply not be atonement for all.

A New Era

After being elected to a second term, Donald Trump will be wholly sold on reestablishing a Christian nation. A nation that values hard work, the ability to come from nothing and do everything. The ability to be a poor schmuck from nowhere and become rich and famous for one little thing, whether a sport, music, or a movie or book or preaching the Word of God. To be a bum and become president. Ok, well that might be stretching it a little.

America used to be that kind of place. Now it's not.

A Christian Nation

We need to rebuild our nation, and Donald Trump, for all his faults is the guy that God touched on the shoulder. Now it is time for us to lift him up and continue living the American dream. The Lord is willing to bring Trump's prophetic destiny to fruition but it requires effort on our part as well. Let's pray together and then hear what God is calling us to address as a nation and as a culture.

A Prayer for a Cultural Change

Lord, we cry out for a shift in culture so great that the devil himself will tremble in America's godly presence. We ask that you change the hearts of men and women across this great country.

We ask that you begin showing our leaders the significance of founding our education and our laws on your Word. And let them see the consequences of a nation that has turned its back on God and begun thinking that man knows best.

Oh Lord! Before it is too late, let us call upon your power, mercy, and forgiveness to turn the cultural attitudes of this country back to You.

Then, we will truly begin to make America great again.

Chapter 11

Daily Decrees for Donald Trump and America

Thou shalt also decree a thing, and it shall be established unto thee: and the light shall shine upon thy ways.
Job 22:28

Donald Trump
I decree in Jesus' name to pray for our leaders and to have my faith strengthened and empowered through prayer and fasting for our country. In the name of the Father, I will sacrifice bodily comfort to come to know God's presence and desires for His people on a more intimate level. Praise be to the Father!

Prophesy
I decree that I will prophesy in the Spirit of Jesus and God the Father all that the Holy Spirit lays upon my heart and for as long as He commands it. I will obey God and lift up this nation and her principles rather than tear them down with negative commentary. I will keep my thoughts and words focused on the Lord's will and God's Word.

Media

I will use Godly discernment in deciding what media outlets to trust in disseminating information regarding national politics and Donald Trump. I decree to follow God's will in edifying fellow believers instead of arguing with them over differing political views, while standing firm in my own.

Faith

Though it may be unpopular, I decree my support and faith in Christ's love and sacrifice and remain unwavering in my belief in His promises. There is no miracle too big for God and that includes seeing Donald Trump come to the Lord and America restore her Christian foundation.

Confidence

Staying in God's Word, I decree that I am safe. I have a lighthouse in Scripture, a home in the loving words and promises of Jesus and I shall not fear evil.

Peace

I decree that my worries flee and dissipate in the sweet presence of the Holy Spirit and no matter what the political climate or outcome of the election, I have a friend that sticks closer than a brother.

God's Presence

I pray and decree that I will live in awareness of God's omnipresent nature and bask in the reality of

His presence on a moment-by-moment level. I will praise Him and enjoy His handiwork all around me and this will keep me from being pulled too far into the cares of this world and the political stage in America.

Gratitude
When I do fear for America's future and for my children's generation of Christians in our nation, I will rest in the Lord's promises of faithfulness and mercy. I decree my gratitude for the beauty of God's saving grace that will continually outweigh my concerns of this earth.

Goodwill
I decree my intent to always be a blessing to people I encounter. Lord, I pray you will highlight the opportunities each day where I can edify and lift another person up. I decree my desire to only speak positivity regardless of how my day is going.

Supreme Court
I decree that Trump will continue to appoint judges to the Supreme Court who will overturn ungodly decisions and use spiritual guidance in establishing the laws of the nation. I pray for wisdom for our Supreme Court justices and peace for them as they make important choices in cases that affect the nation's culture and generations to come.

Patience

Lord, I pray for the patience to wait on Your timing and not make hasty decisions or become overly frustrated when positive change does not happen quickly enough. I decree that I will live a life marked by patience as I do my best to steward the gifts and opportunities I've been given on earth while looking forward to going to my home in Heaven.

Joy

I decree to overcome feelings of despair through Your power, dear Lord. I will live a life of joy and gratitude no matter what the outcome of the election, the status of my finances, or the condition of my health. I decree a season of joy be in front of me and around me throughout my days on this earth.

Forgiveness

I decree a spirit of forgiveness that covers the Body of Christ and by extension, America in this upcoming season of change and spiritual warfare. We will stand and fight for our beliefs, but we will not be overcome or motivated by malice. We will choose to forgive even as Christ has forgiven us. Amen.

Chapter 12

The Power of the Name
By Smith Wigglesworth

Read Acts 3:1-16

All things are possible through the name of Jesus.
God hath highly exalted Him, and given Him the
name, which is above every name, that at the name of
Jesus every knee should bow.

There is power to overcome everything in the world
through the name of Jesus. I am looking forward to a
wonderful union through the name of Jesus. There is
none other name under heaven given among men,
whereby we must be saved. I want to instill into you a
sense of the power, the virtue and the glory of that
name.

Six people went into the house of a sick man to pray
for him. He was an Episcopal vicar, and lay in bed
utterly helpless, without even strength to help
himself. He had read a little tract about healing and
had heard about people praying for the sick, and sent
for these friends, who, he thought, could pray the
prayer of faith. He was anointed according to James

5:14, but, because he had no immediate manifestation of healing, he wept bitterly.

The six people walked out of the room, somewhat crestfallen to see the man lying there in an unchanged condition. When they were outside, one of the six said, "There is one thing we might have done. I wish you would all go back with me and try it."

Put Your Focus on Jesus, Not Sickness

They went back and all got together in a group. This brother said, "Let us whisper the name of Jesus." At first when they whispered this worthy name nothing seemed to happen. But as they continued to whisper, "Jesus! Jesus! Jesus!" the power began to fall.

As they saw that God was beginning to work, their faith and joy increased, and they whispered the name louder and louder. As they did so the man arose from his bed and dressed himself.

The secret was just this, those six people had gotten their eyes off the sick man, and **they were just taken up with the Lord Jesus Himself, and their faith grasped the power that there is in His name**.

Oh, if people would only appreciate the power that there is in this name, there is no telling what would happen. I know that through His name and through the power of His name we have access to God.

The Presence of the Lord

The very face of Jesus fills the whole place with glory. All over the world there are people magnifying that name, and oh, what a joy it is for me to utter it.

One day I went up into the mountain to pray. I had a wonderful day. It was one of the high mountains of Wales. I heard of one man going up this mountain to pray, and the Spirit of the Lord met him so wonderfully that his face shone like that of an angel when he returned. Everyone in the village was talking about it.

As I went up to this mountain and spent the day in the presence of the Lord, His wonderful power seemed to envelop and saturate and fill me.

Raise Lazarus!

Two years before this time there had come to our house two lads from Wales. They were just ordinary lads, but they became very zealous for God. They came to our mission and saw some of the works of God. They said to me, "We would not be surprised if the Lord brings you down to Wales to raise our Lazarus."

They explained that the leader of their assembly was a man who had spent his days working in a tin mine and his nights preaching, and the result was that he had collapsed, gone into consumption, and for four years he had been a helpless invalid, having to be fed with a spoon. While I was up on that mountain top I was reminded of the transfiguration scene, and I felt that the Lord's only purpose in taking us into the glory was to fit us for greater usefulness in the valley.

"The living God has chosen us for His divine inheritance, and He it is who is preparing us for our ministry, that it may be of God and not of man."

"Do You Think We Believe This?"

As I was on the mountain top that day, the Lord said to me, "I want you to go and raise Lazarus." I told the brother who accompanied me of this, and when we got down to the valley, I wrote a postcard:

"When I was up on the mountain praying today, God told me that I was to go and raise Lazarus." I addressed the postcard to the man in the place whose name had been given to me by the two lads. When we arrived at the place we went to the man to whom I had addressed the card. He looked at me and said, "Did you send this?"

I said, "Yes."

He said, "Do you think we believe in this? Here, take it."

And he threw it at me. The man called a servant and said, "Take this man and show him Lazarus." Then he said to me, "The moment you see him you will be ready to go home. Nothing will hold you."

Everything he said was true from the natural viewpoint. The man was helpless. He was nothing but a mass of bones with skin stretched over them. There was no life to be seen. Everything in him spoke of decay.

I said to him, "Will you shout? You remember that at Jericho the people shouted while the walls were still up. God has like victory for you if you will only believe." But I could not get him to believe. There was not an atom of faith there. He had made up his mind not to have anything. It is a blessed thing to learn that God's word can never fail. Never hearken to human plans. God can work mightily when you persist in believing Him in spite of discouragements from the human standpoint.

When I got back to the man to whom I had sent the postcard, he asked, "Are you ready to go now?" I am not moved by what I see. I am moved only by what I believe. I know this — no man looks at appearances if he believes. No man considers how he feels if he believes. The man who believes God has it.

Every man who comes into the Pentecostal condition can laugh at all things and believe God. There is something in the Pentecostal work that is different from anything else in the world. Somehow, in Pentecost, you know that God is a reality. Wherever the Holy Ghost has right of way, the gifts of the Spirit will be in manifestation; and where these gifts are never in manifestation, I question whether He is present.

Pentecostal people are spoiled for anything else than Pentecostal meetings. We want none of the entertainments that the churches are offering. When God comes in He entertains us Himself. Entertained by the King of kings and Lord of lords! Oh, it is wonderful.

There were difficult conditions in that Welsh village, and it seemed impossible to get the people to believe. "Ready to go home?" I was asked. But a man and a woman there asked us to come and stay with them.

Pray and Believe!

I said, "I want to know how many of you people can pray."

No one wanted to pray. I asked if I could get seven people to pray with me for the poor man's deliverance. I said to the two people who were going to entertain us, "I will count on you two, and there is my friend and myself, and we need three others."

I told the people that I trusted that some of them would awaken to their privilege and come in the morning and join us in prayer for the raising of Lazarus. It will never do to give way to human opinions. If God says a thing, you are to believe it.

I told the people that I would not eat anything that night. When I got to bed it seemed as if the devil tried to place on me everything that he had placed on that poor man in the bed. When I awoke I had a cough and all the weakness of a tubercular patient. I rolled out of bed on to the floor and cried out to God to deliver me from the power of the devil. I shouted loud enough to wake everybody in the house, but nobody was disturbed.

Prayer and Fasting

God gave victory, and I got back into bed again as free as ever I was in my life. At 5 o'clock the Lord awakened me and said to me, "Don't break bread until you break it round My table." At six o'clock He gave me these words, "And I will raise him up."

I put my elbow into the fellow who was sleeping with me. He said, "Ugh!" I put my elbow into him again and said, "Do you hear? The Lord says that He will raise him up."

At 8 o'clock they said to me, "Have a little refreshment."

But I have found prayer and fasting the greatest joy, and you will always find it so when you are led by God.

Where Two or Three are Gathered

When we went to the house where Lazarus lived there were eight of us altogether. No one can prove to me that God does not always answer prayer. He always does more than that. He always gives the exceedingly abundant above all we ask or think. I shall never forget how the power of God fell on us as we went into that sick man's room.

Oh, it was lovely! As we circled round the bed I got one brother to hold one of the sick man's hands and I held the other; and we each held the hand of the person next to us.

I said, "We are not going to pray, we are just going to use the name of Jesus." We all knelt down and whispered that one word, "Jesus! Jesus! Jesus!"

The Power of the Name

The power of God fell and then it lifted. Five times the power of God fell and then it remained. But the person who was in the bed was unmoved. Two years previous someone had come along and had tried to raise him up, and the devil had used his lack of success as a means of discouraging Lazarus.

I said, "I don't care what the devil says; if God says he will raise you up it must be so. Forget everything else except what God says about Jesus."

The sixth time the power fell and the sick man's lips began moving and the tears began to fall. I said to him, "The power of God is here; it is yours to accept it."

Repent!

He said, "I have been bitter in my heart, and I know I have grieved the Spirit of God. Here I am helpless. I cannot lift my hands, nor even lift a spoon to my mouth."

I said, "Repent, and God will hear you." He repented and cried out, "O God, let this be to Thy glory!"

As he said this the virtue of the Lord went right through him. I have asked the Lord to never let me tell this story except as it was, for I realize that God cannot bless exaggerations.

As we again said, "Jesus! Jesus! Jesus!" the bed shook, and the man shook. I said to the people that were with me, "You can all go down stairs right away. This is all God. I'm not going to assist him."

Tell Others What God Has Done

I sat and watched that man get up and dress himself. We sang the doxology as he walked down the steps. I said to him, "Now tell what has happened."

It was soon noised abroad that Lazarus had been raised up and the people came from Llanelly and all the district round to see him and hear his testimony. And God brought salvation to many.

This man told right out in the open air what God had done, and as a result many were convicted and converted. All this came through the name of Jesus, through faith in His name, yea, the faith that is by Him gave this sick man perfect soundness in the presence of them all.

Peter and John

Peter and John were helpless, were illiterate, they had no college education. They had been with Jesus. To them had come a wonderful revelation of the power of the name of Jesus. They had handed out the bread and fish after Jesus had multiplied them. They had sat at the table with him and John had often gazed into His face. Peter had often to be rebuked, but Jesus manifested His love to Peter through it all.

Yea, He loved Peter, the wayward one. O, He's a wonderful lover! I have been wayward, I have been stubborn, I had an unmanageable temper at one time, but how patient He has been.

They Had No Money, But They Had the Power of God

I am here to tell you that there is power in Jesus and in his wondrous name to transform anyone, to heal anyone. If you will see Him as God's Lamb, as God's beloved Son who had laid upon Him the iniquity of us all, if only you will see that Jesus paid the whole price for our redemption that we might be free, you can enter into your purchased inheritance of salvation, of life and of power. Poor Peter, and poor John! They had no money!

But they had faith, they had the power of the Holy Ghost, they had God. You can have God even though you have nothing else. Even though you have lost your character you can have God. I have seen the worst men saved by the power of God. I was one day preaching about the name of Jesus and there was a man leaning against a lamppost, listening. It took a lamppost to enable him to keep on his feet.

A Man that God Could Use

We had finished our open-air meeting, and the man was still leaning against the post. I asked him, "Are you sick?" He showed me his hand and I saw beneath his coat, he had a silver handled dagger. He told me that he was on his way to kill his unfaithful wife, but that he had heard me speaking about the power of the name of Jesus and could not get away. He said that he felt just helpless.

I said, "Get you down." And there on the square, with people passing up and down, he got saved. I took him to my home and put on him a new suit. I saw that there was something in that man that God could use.

He said to me the next morning, "God has revealed Jesus to me; I see that all has been laid upon Jesus." I lent him some money, and he soon got together a wonderful little home.

His faithless wife was living with another man, but he invited her back to the home that he had prepared for her. She came: and, where enmity and hatred had been before, the whole situation was transformed by love.

God made that man a minister wherever he went. There is power in the name of Jesus everywhere. God can save to the uttermost.

Dare To Believe

There comes before me a meeting we had in Stockholm that I shall ever bear in mind. There was a home for incurables there and one of the inmates was brought to the meeting. He had palsy and was shaking all over. He stood up before 3,000 people and came to the platform, supported by two others.

The power of God fell on him as I anointed him in the name of Jesus. The moment I touched him he dropped his crutch and began to walk in the name of Jesus. He walked down the steps and round that great building in view of all the people. There is nothing that our God cannot do. He will do everything if you will dare to believe.

Someone said to me, "Will you go to this Home for Incurables?" They took me there on my rest day. They brought out the sick people into a great corridor and in one hour the Lord set about twenty of them free. The name of Jesus is so marvelous.

Rise Up and Walk

Peter and John had no conception of all that was in that name; neither had the man, lame from his mother's womb, who was laid daily at the gate; but they had faith to say, "In the name of Jesus Christ of Nazareth, rise up and walk." And as Peter took him by the right hand, and lifted him up, immediately his feet and anklebones received strength, and he went into the temple with them, walking and leaping and praising God.

How can it be done? Through His name, through faith in His name, through faith which is by Him.

-    Smith Wigglesworth, *Ever Increasing Faith*

A Word in Conclusion

The Lord God has spoken and His word is final. It shall last through the ages. What will we do with it today? What will you do after you've heard and considered this word from the Lord?

Will you just put it away and forget it as if it were just another sermon? Or will you act—will you humble yourself and pray and ask God to show you where you need to repent, ask God to show you where you need to prophesy and heal people?

Don't Grow Weary in Well doing

And let us not be weary in well doing: for in due season we shall reap, if we faint not.
Galations 6:9 (KJV)

As you pray and examine your life internally, and as you prophesy and testify externally, exercise patience and perseverance in this season. The Lord has promised to provide the strength so long as we do not give up.

Please, as we watch Trump's prophetic destiny unfold through the election season and beyond, let us be prayerful. Let us seek the Lord while He may be found. Let us cry out for our own prophetic destiny through Christ Jesus, Amen.

Thank you so much for reading and please take two minutes to leave a review, good, bad or indifferent to help others discern the profitability of this word.

Be blessed,
John Whitman.

*And ye shall know the truth, and
the truth shall make you free*

John 8:32

Other Books by John Whitman

amazon.com/author/johnwhitman

68119531R00067

Made in the USA
Columbia, SC
04 August 2019